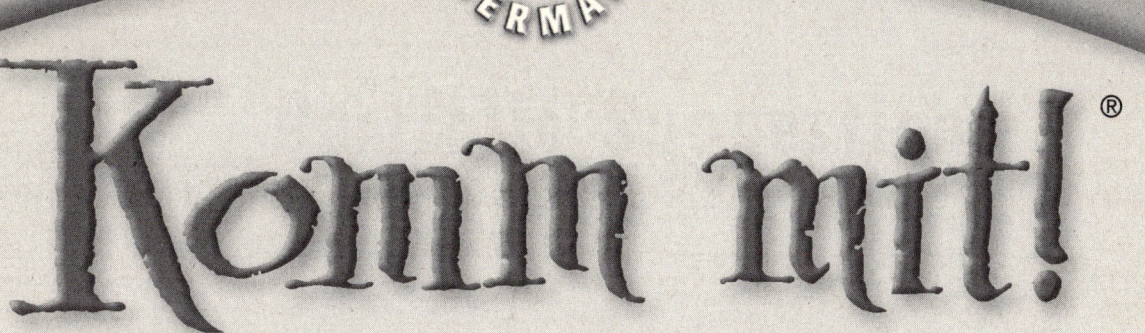

Alternative Assessment Guide

HOLT, RINEHART AND WINSTON

A Harcourt Classroom Education Company

Austin • New York • Orlando • Atlanta • San Francisco • Boston • Dallas • Toronto • London

Contributing Writer

Catherine Dallas Purdy

Copyright © by Holt, Rinehart and Winston

All rights reserved. No part of this publication may be reproduced or transmitted in any form or by any means, electronic or mechanical, including photocopy, recording, or any information storage and retrieval system, without permission in writing from the publisher.

Teachers using KOMM MIT! may photocopy blackline masters in complete pages in sufficient quantities for classroom use only and not for resale.

Cover Photo/Illustration Credits:
Group of students: George Winkler/HRW Photo; paintbrushes: Image Copyright ©2003 Photodisc, Inc.

KOMM MIT! is a trademark licensed to Holt, Rinehart and Winston, registered in the United States of America and/or other jurisdictions.

Printed in the United States of America

ISBN 0-03-065574-9

4 5 6 7   018   05

Contents

To the Teacher .... iv-vi

Rubrics and Evaluation Guidelines

Oral Rubric A 3
Oral Rubric B 4
Oral Progress Report 5
Written Rubric A 6
Written Rubric B 7
Written Progress Report 8
Peer Editing Rubric 9

Portfolio Suggestions

Documentation of Group Work 13
Student's Portfolio Checklist 14
Teacher's Portfolio Checklist 15
Portfolio Self-Evaluation 16
Portfolio Evaluation 17
Chapter 1 18
Chapter 2 19
Chapter 3 20
Chapter 4 21
Chapter 5 22
Chapter 6 23
Chapter 7 24
Chapter 8 25
Chapter 9 26
Chapter 10 27
Chapter 11 28
Chapter 12 29

Performance Assessment

Chapter 1 32
Chapter 2 33
Chapter 3 34
Chapter 4 35
Chapter 5 36
Chapter 6 37
Chapter 7 38
Chapter 8 39
Chapter 9 40
Chapter 10 41
Chapter 11 42
Chapter 12 43

CD-ROM Assessment

Chapter 1 46
Chapter 2 47
Chapter 3 48
Chapter 4 49
Chapter 5 50
Chapter 6 51
Chapter 7 52
Chapter 8 53
Chapter 9 54
Chapter 10 55
Chapter 11 56
Chapter 12 57

To the Teacher

Individual students have individual needs and ways of learning, and progress at different rates in the development of their oral and written skills. The *Alternative Assessment Guide* is designed to accommodate those differences, and to offer opportunities for all students to be evaluated in the most favorable light possible and under circumstances that enable them to succeed.

The *Alternative Assessment Guide* contains information and suggestions for evaluating student progress in three ways that go beyond the standard quizzes and tests: portfolio assessment, performance assessment, and CD-ROM assessment. Each section of the guide contains some general information and specific, chapter-related suggestions for incorporating each type of assessment into your instructional plan.

Portfolio Assessment

Student portfolios are of great benefit to foreign language students and teachers alike because they provide documentation of a student's efforts, progress, and achievements over a given period of time. In addition, students can receive both positive feedback and constructive criticism by sharing their portfolios with teachers, family, and peers. The opportunity for self-reflection provided by using a portfolio encourages students to participate in their learning in a positive way, thus fostering pride, ownership, and self-esteem.

This guide includes a variety of materials that will help you implement and assess student portfolios. The written and oral activity evaluation forms, student and teacher checklists, peer editing rubric, and portfolio evaluation sheets included here are designed for use with student portfolios, or they may be used independently as part of any assessment program.

DETERMINING A PURPOSE

The first step in implementing portfolios in your classroom is to determine their purpose. You can use portfolios to assess the individual student's growth and progress, to make students active in the assessment process, to provide evidence and documentation of students' work for more effective communication with parents, or to evaluate an instructional program of curriculum. Both the contents of this portfolio and the manner in which it is to be evaluated will depend directly on the purpose(s) the portfolio is to serve. Before including any work in their portfolios, students should understand the purpose of the portfolio and the criteria by which their work will be evaluated.

SETTING UP THE PORTFOLIOS

While portfolios can be used to meet various objectives, they are especially useful tools for assessing written and oral work. Written items can assume a variety of formats, including lists, posters, personal correspondence, poems, stories, articles, and essays, depending on the level and needs of the students. Oral items, such as conversations, interviews, commercials, and skits, may be recorded on audio- or videocassette for incorporation into the portfolio. Whatever the format, both written and oral work can include evidence of the developmental process, such as notes taken during brainstorming, outlines, early drafts, or scripts, as well as the finished product.

Each student can be responsible for keeping the materials selected for his or her portfolio. Encourage students to personalize the presentation of their portfolios and to keep in mind that their portfolios may include not only papers, but also audio- and videocassettes and diskettes.

SELECTING MATERIALS FOR THE PORTFOLIO

There are several ways you and your students can select materials to include in portfolios. The portfolio should not be seen as a repository for all student work; items should be selected on the basis of the portfolio's purpose and the evaluation criteria to be used.

Student Selection Many teachers prefer to let students choose samples of their best work to include in their portfolios. Early in the year, you may tell students how many written and oral items to include in their portfolios (for example, one written and one oral item per chapter) and allow students the freedom to choose those pieces that they feel best represent their ability in the language. In this case, the written and oral portfolio items suggested in this guide would be treated as any other writing or speaking activities, and students would decide whether or not to include these in their portfolios. This option empowers students by placing control of specific content in their hands. The feeling of ownership of the portfolio is likely to increase as the students' involvement at the decision-making level increases.

Teacher-Directed Selection Some teachers prefer to maintain portfolios that contain students' responses to specific prompts or activities. The oral and written portfolio items suggested in this guide, or other writing or speaking activities of your choice, could be assigned specifically for inclusion in the portfolio. This type of portfolio allows you to focus attention on particular functions, vocabulary items, and grammar points.

Collaborative Selection A third option combines the two approaches described above. You can assign specific activities from which students may choose a predetermined number of assignments to include in their portfolios, or you can assign some specific activities and allow the students to choose others on their own. The collaborative approach allows you to focus on particular objectives while at the same time granting students the opportunity to showcase what they perceive as their best work.

As the classroom teacher, you are in the best position to decide what type of portfolio is most beneficial to your program and students. The most important step is deciding what objectives and outcomes the portfolio should assess, and then assigning or helping students select items that will best reflect those objectives and outcomes.

CHAPTER-SPECIFIC PORTFOLIO SUGGESTIONS

Specific portfolio suggestions, one written and one oral, are provided for each chapter. These suggestions are based on existing *Pupil's Edition* activities that have been expanded to incorporate most of the functions and vocabulary for each chapter. These materials may be included in the students' portfolios or used as guidelines for the inclusion of other materials.

USING THE PORTFOLIO CHECKLISTS

Regardless of the method of material selection you choose, the checklists on pages 14 and 15 will help you and your students keep the portfolios organized. The *Student's Portfolio Checklist* is designed to help students track the items they include. The *Teacher's Portfolio Checklist* is a running list of the items you expect students to include. If you choose to allow students to select materials for their portfolios, your checklist will be very general, specifying only the types of items and the dates on which each should be included. Your checklist will be more specific if you are assigning particular portfolio activities, as it should list these and the dates on which they are to appear.

PEER EDITING

Peer editing provides students with an opportunity to help each other develop their writing skills. It also promotes an atmosphere of responsibility and teamwork throughout the writing process. We have included a *Peer Editing Rubric* to encourage peer editing in the classroom and to aid students in this part of the evaluation process. Using the rubric, students can exchange compositions (usually a first draft) and edit each other's work according to a clearly designed step-by-step process. The rubric is divided into three parts. Part I helps students examine the overall content of the written assignment using specific question prompts concerning vocabulary, organization, and comprehensibility. Part II helps students examine grammar and mechanics. You can use this section to focus student editors' attention on particular functions and grammar points presented in each chapter. For example, in Chapter 2 you might choose to focus on proper word order. Use the space labeled "Target Functions and Grammar" in the *Peer Editing Rubric* for this purpose. Part III asks students to discuss the first two parts of the rubric, in order to encourage them to evaluate each other's work critically. Even though the rubric is organized in this step-by-step manner, your help in addressing students' questions will further increase the effectiveness of the peer editing process. The *Peer Editing Rubric* can be used with any written assignment.

DOCUMENTING GROUP WORK

Very often a group-work project cannot be included in an individual's portfolio because of its size or the difficulties involved in making copies for each group member (posters, bulletin boards, videos, etc.). Other group or pair activities, such as conversations or skits, cannot be included in the portfolio unless they are recorded. To help students document such activities in their portfolios, you may want to use the form *Documentation of Group Work* found on page 13.

EVALUATING THE TOTAL PORTFOLIO

The methods you use to evaluate your students' total portfolios, as well as the frequency with which you do so, will depend upon the stated purpose. Ideally, students' portfolios should be evaluated at regular intervals over the course of the academic year. You should establish the length of the assessment period in advance — six weeks, a quarter, a semester, etc. The *Portfolio Self-Evaluation* and *Portfolio Evaluation* forms on pages 16 and 17 are designed to aid you and your students in assessing the portfolio at the end of each established period. In order to ensure that portfolios are being successfully maintained, you might want to meet individually with each student throughout each assessment period. In addition, individual conferences with students should be scheduled at the end of each evaluation period to discuss their portfolios and compare your assessment with their own. For further information about portfolio assessment, see pages T40-41 of the ***Komm mit!*** *Annotated Teacher's Edition*.

Performance Assessment

Performance assessment provides an alternative to traditional testing methods by using authentic situations as contexts for performing communicative, competency-based tasks. For every chapter of the *Pupil's Edition,* this guide provides performance assessment suggestions to go with each **Stufe** of the chapter, and one suggestion for global performance assessment that involves vocabulary and functions located throughout the chapter. These suggestions give students the opportunity to demonstrate acquired language proficiency and cultural competence in interviews, conversations, dialogues, or skits that can be performed for the entire class, or recorded or videotaped for evaluation at a later time. Performance assessment recordings can be included in student portfolios or used independently, according to your oral evaluation needs.

CD-ROM Assessment

The ***Komm mit!*** *Interactive CD-ROM Tutor* provides a unique tool for evaluating students' language proficiency and for incorporating technology in the classroom. CD-ROM technology appeals to a variety of student learning styles and offers you an efficient means by which to gauge student progress. This guide provides instruction for written activities, such as lists, letters, e-mail, journal entries, and advertisements. Oral activities include conversations, interviews, and dialogues. Writing and recording features also enable you to create your own activities and to evaluate student work according to your needs. Student work can be saved to a disk and included in students' portfolios. For instructions on how to use CD-ROM for assessment, log on to **www.hrw.com/CDROMTUTOR**.

Rubrics and Evaluation Guidelines

Name _____ Class _____ Date _____

 Oral Rubric A

Use the following criteria to evaluate oral assignments. For assignments for which comprehension is difficult to evaluate, you might want to give students full credit for comprehension or weigh other categories more heavily.

	4	**3**	**2**	**1**
Content	Complete	Generally complete	Somewhat complete	Incomplete
	Speaker consistently uses the appropriate functions and vocabulary necessary to communicate.	Speaker usually uses the appropriate functions and vocabulary necessary to communicate.	Speaker sometimes uses the appropriate functions and vocabulary necessary to communicate.	Speaker uses few of the appropriate functions and vocabulary necessary to communicate.
Comprehension	Total comprehension	General comprehension	Moderate comprehension	Little comprehension
	Speaker understands all of what is said to him or her.	Speaker understands most of what is said to him or her.	Speaker understands some of what is said to him or her.	Speaker understands little of what is said to him or her.
Comprehensibility	Comprehensible	Usually comprehensible	Sometimes comprehensible	Seldom comprehensible
	Listener always understands what the speaker is trying to communicate.	Listener understands most of what the speaker is trying to communicate.	Listener understands less than half of what the speaker is trying to communicate.	Listener understands little of what the speaker is trying to communicate.
Accuracy	Accurate	Usually accurate	Sometimes accurate	Seldom accurate
	Speaker uses language correctly, including grammar, vocabulary, and word order.	Speaker usually uses language correctly, including grammar, vocabulary, and word order.	Speaker has some problems with language usage.	Speaker makes many errors in language usage.
Fluency	Fluent	Moderately fluent	Somewhat fluent	Not fluent
	Speaker speaks clearly without hesitation. Pronunciation and intonation sound natural.	Speaker has few problems with hesitation, pronunciation, and/or intonation.	Speaker has some problems with hesitation, pronunciation, and/or intonation.	Speaker hesitates frequently and struggles with pronunciation and intonation.

German 1 Komm mit!

Copyright © by Holt, Rinehart and Winston. All rights reserved.

Name _____ Class _____ Date _____

Oral Rubric B

Assignment _____

Targeted function(s) _____

_____

Targeted vocabulary _____

Targeted grammar _____

Content	You used the functions and vocabulary necessary to communicate.	(Excellent)	4	3	2	1	(Poor)
Comprehension	You understood what was said to you and responded appropriately.	(Excellent)	4	3	2	1	(Poor)
Comprehensibility	The listener was able to understand what you were trying to communicate.	(Excellent)	4	3	2	1	(Poor)
Accuracy	You used language correctly, including grammar, vocabulary, and word order.	(Excellent)	4	3	2	1	(Poor)
Fluency	You spoke clearly and without hesitation. Your pronunciation and intonation sounded natural.	(Excellent)	4	3	2	1	(Poor)

Total Score _____

Comments _____

_____

_____

_____

Name _____ Class _____ Date _____

 **Oral Progress Report**

OVERALL IMPRESSION
☐ Excellent   ☐ Good   ☐ Satisfactory   ☐ Unsatisfactory

Some aspects of this item that are particularly good are _____
_____
_____
_____
_____

Some areas that could be improved are _____
_____
_____
_____
_____

To improve your speaking, I recommend _____
_____
_____
_____
_____

Additional Comments:
_____
_____
_____
_____

Name _____ Class _____ Date _____

Written Rubric A

Use the following criteria to evaluate written assignments.

	4	**3**	**2**	**1**
Content	Complete	Generally complete	Somewhat complete	Incomplete
	Writer uses the appropriate functions and vocabulary for the topic.	Writer usually uses the appropriate functions and vocabulary for the topic.	Writer uses few of the appropriate functions and vocabulary for the topic.	Writer uses none of the appropriate functions and vocabulary for the topic.
Comprehensibility	Comprehensible	Usually comprehensible	Sometimes comprehensible	Seldom comprehensible
	Reader can always understand what the writer is trying to communicate.	Reader can understand most of what the writer is trying to communicate.	Reader can understand less than half of what the writer is trying to communicate.	Reader can understand little of what the writer is trying to communicate.
Accuracy	Accurate	Usually accurate	Sometimes accurate	Seldom accurate
	Writer uses language correctly, including grammar, spelling, word order, and punctuation.	Writer usually uses language correctly, including grammar, spelling, word order, and punctuation.	Writer has some problems with language usage.	Writer makes a significant number of errors in language usage.
Organization	Well-organized	Generally well-organized	Somewhat organized	Poorly organized
	Presentation is logical and effective.	Presentation is generally logical and effective with a few minor problems.	Presentation is somewhat illogical and confusing in places.	Presentation lacks logical order and organization.
Effort	Excellent effort	Good effort	Moderate effort	Minimal effort
	Writer exceeds the requirements of the assignment and has put care and effort into the process.	Writer fulfills all of the requirements of the assignment.	Writer fulfills some of the requirements of the assignment.	Writer fulfills few of the requirements of the assignment.

Alternative Assessment Guide

German 1 Komm mit!

Copyright © by Holt, Rinehart and Winston. All rights reserved.

Name _____ Class _____ Date _____

 **Written Rubric B**

Assignment _____

Targeted function(s) _____
_____

Targeted vocabulary _____

Targeted grammar _____

Content	You used the functions and vocabulary necessary to communicate.	(Excellent)	4	3	2	1	(Poor)
Comprehensibility	The reader was able to understand what you were trying to communicate.	(Excellent)	4	3	2	1	(Poor)
Accuracy	You used language correctly, including grammar, spelling, word order, and punctuation.	(Excellent)	4	3	2	1	(Poor)
Organization	Your presentation was logical and effective.	(Excellent)	4	3	2	1	(Poor)
Effort	You put a lot of thought and effort into this assignment.	(Excellent)	4	3	2	1	(Poor)

Total Score _____

Comments _____
_____
_____
_____

German 1 Komm mit!   Alternative Assessment Guide **7**

Name _____ Class _____ Date _____

 Written Progress Report

OVERALL IMPRESSION
☐ Excellent   ☐ Good   ☐ Satisfactory   ☐ Unsatisfactory

Some aspects of this item that are particularly good are _____
_____
_____
_____
_____

Some areas that could be improved are _____
_____
_____
_____
_____

To improve your written work, I recommend _____
_____
_____
_____
_____
_____

Additional Comments:
_____
_____
_____
_____
_____

8 Alternative Assessment Guide

German 1 Komm mit!

Copyright © by Holt, Rinehart and Winston. All rights reserved.

Name _____ Class _____ Date _____

Peer Editing Rubric

Chapter _____

I. Content: Look for the following elements in your partner's compositions. Put a check next to each category when you finish it.

1. _____ Vocabulary — Does the composition use enough new vocabulary from the chapter? Underline all the new vocabulary words you find from this chapter. What additional words do you suggest that your partner use?

2. _____ Organization — Is the composition organized and easy to follow? Can you find an introduction and a conclusion?

3. _____ Comprehensibility — Is the composition clear and easy to understand? Is there a specific part that was hard to understand? Did you understand the author's meaning? Draw a box around any sections that were particularly hard to understand.

4. _____ Target Functions and Grammar — Ask your teacher what parts of language you should focus on for this chapter and list them below.

Focus: _____

II. Proofreader's checklist: Circle any errors you find in your partner's composition. See the chart below for some examples.

Subject – Verb Agreement	Er (komme) aus München. *kommt*
Article/Pronoun/ Use of Correct Case	(Die) Mädchen wohnt in der Nähe. *Das* Der Schrank ist alt. (Es) ist auch groß. *Er* Er gibt (seine) Schwester (ein) Blumenstrauß. *seiner / einen*
Spelling	Der Junge ist (funfzehn) Jahre alt. *fünfzehn*
Word Order	Heute (die Gabi kommt) mit dem Bus. *kommt die Gabi* Ich glaube, dass er (hat eine Schwester). *eine Schwester hat.*
Capitalization/Punctuation	Ich lese gern (romane). *Romane* Ich bleibe zu Hause weil ich Hausaufgaben mache. *Hause,*
Word Choice	Ich (gehe) mit dem Auto. *fahre*

III. Explain your content and grammar suggestions to your partner. Answer any questions about the edits.

Peer Editor's signature: _____ Date: _____

German 1 Komm mit! — Alternative Assessment Guide

Portfolio Suggestions

Name _____ Class _____ Date _____

 Documentation of Group Work

Item _____ Chapter _____

Group Members: _____
_____
_____
_____
_____
_____
_____

Description of Item: _____
_____
_____
_____
_____
_____
_____
_____

Personal Contribution: _____
_____
_____
_____
_____
_____
_____
_____
_____

Please rate your personal contribution to the group's work.
☐ Excellent ☐ Good ☐ Satisfactory ☐ Unsatisfactory

German 1 Komm mit!   Alternative Assessment Guide

Copyright © by Holt, Rinehart and Winston. All rights reserved.

Name _____ Class _____ Date _____

 Student's Portfolio Checklist

To the Student This form should be used to keep track of the materials you are including in your portfolio. It is important that you keep this list up-to-date so that your portfolio will be complete at the end of the assessment period. As you build your portfolio, try to include pieces of your work that demonstrate progress in your ability to speak and write in German.

	Type of Item	Date Completed	Date Placed in Portfolio
Item #1			
Item #2			
Item #3			
Item #4			
Item #5			
Item #6			
Item #7			
Item #8			
Item #9			
Item #10			
Item #11			
Item #12			

Teacher's Portfolio Checklist

To the Teacher This form should be used to keep track of the materials you expect your students to keep in their portfolios for the semester. Encourage students to keep their lists up-to-date so that their portfolios will be complete at the end of the assessment period.

	Type of Item	Date Assigned	Date Due in Portfolio
Item #1			
Item #2			
Item #3			
Item #4			
Item #5			
Item #6			
Item #7			
Item #8			
Item #9			
Item #10			
Item #11			
Item #12			

German 1 Komm mit!   Alternative Assessment Guide

Name _____ Class _____ Date _____

 Portfolio Self-Evaluation

To the Student Your portfolio consists of selections of your written and oral work. You should consider all the items in your portfolio as you evaluate your progress. Read the statements below and mark the box to the right of each statement that shows how well your portfolio demonstrates your skills and abilities in German.

	Strongly Agree	Agree	Disagree	Strongly Disagree
1. My portfolio contains all of the required items.				
2. My portfolio provides evidence of my progress in speaking and writing German.				
3. The items in my portfolio demonstrate that I can communicate my ideas in German.				
4. The items in my portfolio demonstrate accurate use of German.				
5. The items in my portfolio show that I understand and can use a wide variety of vocabulary.				
6. When creating the items in my portfolio, I tried to use what I have learned in new ways.				
7. The items in my portfolio provide an accurate picture of my skills and abilities in German.				

My favorite item in my portfolio is _____

because (please give at least three reasons) _____

_____

_____

_____

_____

_____

_____

In assessing my overall portfolio, I find it to be (check one):

☐ Excellent ☐ Good ☐ Satisfactory ☐ Unsatisfactory

16 Alternative Assessment Guide   German 1 Komm mit!

Copyright © by Holt, Rinehart and Winston. All rights reserved.

Student's Name _____ Class _____

 Portfolio Evaluation

To the Student I have reviewed the items in your portfolio and want to share with you my reactions to your work.

Teacher's Signature _____

Date _____

	Strongly Agree	Agree	Disagree	Strongly Disagree
1. Your portfolio contains all of the required items.				
2. Your portfolio provides evidence of your progress in speaking and writing German.				
3. The items in your portfolio demonstrate that you can communicate your ideas in German.				
4. The items in your portfolio demonstrate accurate use of German.				
5. The items in your portfolio demonstrate the use of a wide variety of German vocabulary.				
6. When creating the items in your portfolio, you have tried to use what you have learned in new ways.				
7. The items in your portfolio provide an accurate picture of your skills and abilities in German.				

My favorite item in your portfolio is _____

because _____

_____

_____

One area in which you seem to need improvement is _____

_____

For your next portfolio collection, I would like to suggest _____

_____

In assessing your overall portfolio, I find it to be:

☐ Excellent   ☐ Good   ☐ Satisfactory   ☐ Unsatisfactory

Wer bist du?

Portfolio Suggestions

Written: Activity 20

Expanded Activity Students should imagine they have met several German-speaking exchange students who don't know English yet. The German teacher has invited both groups of students to a party. The Americans want to make a good impression and be able to introduce their new friends to the teacher in German, telling their names, ages, and hometowns. Instruct the students to write on an index card the questions they will need to ask to get this information. They should then interview the other students and write the answers on index cards.

Purpose To practice writing simple questions and answers in German. The targeted functions are asking someone's name and age and telling yours, and talking about where people are from.

Rationale Applying the targeted functional expressions to a real-life situation helps students recognize that they are learning language for communication. Writing these expressions in a real-life context also helps students to internalize the expressions.

Materials Each student will need at least two 3 x 5-inch index cards.

Portfolio Item Students should put the index cards with interview questions and answers into their portfolios. Taping the index cards to a 8 1/2 x 11-inch piece of paper may make storage easier.

Oral: Anwendung Activity 2

The oral activity is a continuation of the written activity described above. The two can be done sequentially, or the oral activity can be done later.

Expanded Activity Students will use the information obtained in their interviews to make introductions at the "party." Be sure the students have memorized the information written on their cards, since they will not be able to use them while playing their roles. Create a "party area" in the classroom by arranging chairs around an empty space. Use the door of the classroom as the front door of the teacher's residence. Have some students already at the "party," and others in the hall ready to arrive. Arriving at the party, the students exchange greetings and introduce the newcomers to their friends and to the teacher, telling the name, age, and hometown of each person. After introductions have been made, have the two groups of students switch roles and start over.

Purpose To practice making introductions. The targeted functions are saying hello and goodbye, asking someone's name and giving yours, asking someone's age and giving yours, and talking about where people are from.

Rationale Simulating real situations helps students activate the language, thus accelerating their learning.

Materials For incorporation into students' portfolios, you will need audio or video equipment to record the activity and individual cassettes or a class master.

Portfolio Item Record the "party" on audio- or videocassette for incorporation into students' portfolios.

Spiel und Spaß

Portfolio Suggestions

Written: Activity 18

Expanded Activity Students brainstorm as a class to create 10 questions in German that they might ask a famous singer or actor about his or her activities and interests. Each student should write each question at the top of a different page, leaving room for answers. Students then get into pairs to conduct their interviews, which can be recorded and used as an oral portfolio item. One student plays the role of a real or imaginary star, while the other plays the reporter. The reporter notes the star's answers in German. Students then switch roles so both get a chance to interview and be interviewed. For homework have students write a short paragraph (5-10 sentences) summarizing the interests and activities of the star they interviewed. During the next class day, have the students exchange papers with a partner and proofread each other's paragraphs. They can discuss any corrections with each other and, if necessary, with the teacher. Have students rewrite their paragraphs for homework.

Purpose To practice writing questions and noting answers in an interview context. The targeted functions are talking about interests, expressing likes and dislikes, and saying when you do various activities.

Rationale Students are more likely to learn new vocabulary when they believe it is relevant to their lives.

Materials No special materials are necessary.

Portfolio Item Students should include their interview notes as well as the first and second drafts of their paragraphs in their portfolios.

Oral: Anwendung Activity 6

The written portfolio item suggested above for Chapter 2 can be adapted as an oral portfolio activity.

Expanded Activity After the class has brainstormed together to come up with the interview questions, pairs of students take on the roles of reporter and star to conduct their interviews.

Purpose To practice asking and responding to questions in the context of an interview. The targeted functions are talking about interests, expressing likes and dislikes, and saying when you do various activities.

Rationale Language skills are not isolated in life. We don't only talk; we talk and listen or listen and write, etc. For this reason, skills should not be practiced in isolation, but combined whenever possible.

Materials Students will need tape recorders and cassette tapes on which to record their interviews.

Portfolio Item Each reporter should record his or her interview on audio cassette to be incorporated into the portfolio.

German 1 Komm mit!   Alternative Assessment Guide **19**

Komm mit nach Hause!

Portfolio Suggestions

Written: Zum Lesen Activity 7a

Expanded Activity Each student writes a short classified ad in German describing the apartment he or she wishes to rent (or share) for a year's study in Germany. (Refer students to pages 82 and 83 for models of classified ads.) Collect the ads and redistribute them. Each student now assumes the role of a person wishing to lease (or share) an apartment and writes a letter responding to the ad he or she has received.

Purpose To transfer what students learned in the reading selection for Chapter 3. To practice creating classified ads and responding in writing with appropriate vocabulary.

Rationale Creating their own ads will encourage students to familiarize themselves more fully with authentic advertisements.

Materials No special materials are necessary.

Portfolio Item In order to show that a true correspondence has occurred, students should include their own classified ad as well as a photocopy of the letter they received in response to their ad.

Oral: Anwendung Activity 1

Expanded Activity The entire class works together to create a list of food and drinks that are likely to be offered to a guest in a given situation (for an afternoon snack, lunch, dinner, etc.). These words are written on the board. Review the functional expressions for offering something to eat and drink, responding to an offer, and saying please, thank you, and you're welcome. Divide students into groups of three. Have each group write the food and drink vocabulary words from the board on small slips of paper, fold them, and put them into a container. One person in each group is "it" and draws a word from the container. The other two students in the group take turns offering possible refreshments from the words on the board. Each time they offer an item that is not written on the paper, "it" must refuse politely. When the correct item is offered, "it" accepts and another group member becomes "it."

Purpose To practice various ways of offering and refusing refreshment. The targeted functions are offering something to eat and drink and responding to an offer, and saying please, thank you, and you're welcome.

Rationale Making offers and accepting or refusing them politely are part of everyone's automatic language skills in their native language. With practice, these expressions will become automatic in the second language as well.

Materials Each group will need small slips of paper and some sort of container. You will also need audio or video equipment and cassettes.

Portfolio Item Record at least one turn of each group for incorporation into students' portfolios.

Alles für die Schule!

Portfolio Suggestions

Written: Anwendung Activity 6

Expanded Activity Students will correspond in groups of 3. Each student writes a letter to a friend (A writes to B, B writes to C, C writes to A) telling about life at school (favorite classes, friends, etc.) and detailing their schedules. Students exchange letters. Recipients jot down the information in the letter and exchange again. Each student jots down the information in the second letter. Having heard from two pen pals, each student then writes a letter to a fourth person outside the group (the teacher) telling about the school experiences of the two friends and adding information about the writer's own schedule.

Purpose To practice writing about schedules and times, to communicate schedules, and to synthesize information from different sources and report it. The targeted functions are talking about class schedules, using a schedule to talk about time, sequencing events, and expressing likes, dislikes, and favorites.

Rationale Being able to communcate schedules and sequence events is essential as people juggle and coordinate all they have to do.

Materials No special materials are necessary.

Portfolio Item In the portfolio each student should include the two letters he or she wrote, as well as photocopies of the two letters he or she received.

Oral: Activity 13

Expanded Activity If they haven't already done so, have students write out their schedules in German and be prepared to talk about them in class. For additional practice and review, students should also include a schedule of their extracurricular activities. Have the whole class work together to brainstorm questions they will need to ask in order to get the information necessary to complete a partner's class and activity schedule. Then divide students into pairs and have them conduct the interviews.

Purpose To practice talking about schedules for classes and extracurricular actvities. The targeted functions are talking about class schedules, using a schedule to talk about time, and sequencing events.

Rationale Having students develop questions together allows each to benefit from the others' knowledge before producing language individually.

Materials Students will need paper and blank class schedules. In addition, you will need audio or video equipment and cassettes.

Portfolio Item Record the interaction between pairs on audio- or videocassette for incorporation into portfolios.

German 1 Komm mit! Alternative Assessment Guide

Kapitel 5: Klamotten kaufen

Portfolio Suggestions

Written: Activity 22

Expanded Activity Have students bring some clothing items to class. After arranging the clothes as if they were in a boutique with price and size tags, the whole class works together to write a conversation among three people (two shoppers and a sales clerk) at a fashionable boutique. The conversation should include as many of the functional expressions covered in the chapter as possible. Before beginning the conversation, divide students into three groups. Give each group a focus (functions, grammar, vocabulary) for which they are primarily responsible. While the whole class will work together to write the conversation, the grammar group will pay special attention to word order, verb endings, etc.; the function group will make sure functions are used correctly and appropriately; and the vocabulary group will be responsible for incorporating a wide range of vocabulary. With input from the three groups, correct the conversation as you go.

Purpose To write a sustained conversation. The targeted functions are expressing wishes when shopping, commenting on and describing clothes, giving compliments and responding to them, and talking about trying on clothes.

Rationale Conversations for beginners tend to be short and grammatically flawed. By writing and correcting a conversation before role-playing it, students have a chance to use more vocabulary and more accurate grammar than they would otherwise spontaneously use.

Materials Each student should bring an item of clothing to class to create a "boutique." They will also need paper and pins to make price and size tags, an improvised display space on which to arrange the items for sale, and hangers and a rack on which to hang the clothing.

Portfolio Item Each student should write down the conversation for incorporation into individual portfolios.

Oral: Activity 28

Expanded Activity Have students in groups of three create TV commercials using the clothing, boutique setting, and conversation created for the written activity. Each group can adjust the conversation as they see fit to make it appropriate for a TV advertisement. For example, students may want to use more descriptive adjectives to emphasize the beauty, selection of styles, and price more emphatically than they would in a normal conversation. Give students time to prepare and practice their commercials before performing them.

Purpose To practice the functions and vocabulary from this chapter in a creative and entertaining way. The targeted functions are expressing wishes when shopping, commenting on and describing clothes, giving compliments and responding to them, and talking about trying on clothes.

Rationale Students will enjoy the opportunity to step beyond everyday language and to use German more creatively.

Materials You will need audio or video equipment and cassettes.

Portfolio Item Record students' commercials on audio- or videocassette for incorporation into their portfolios.

Pläne machen

Portfolio Suggestions

Written: Zum Lesen Activity 6c

Expanded Activity Tell students that they are visiting Hamburg or another German city and that they are going to write a postcard to a friend describing their plans for the weekend. Students first brainstorm a list of activities they would like to do over the weekend, and then write the first draft of their postcard. After they have written the first draft, students should exchange their papers for peer editing. Students write their final copy on 5 x 8-inch index cards which they have decorated to resemble a postcard.

Purpose To transfer what students used in the reading activity. The targeted function is making plans.

Rationale Students need to learn to approach writing as a process.

Materials Students will need paper, 5 x 8-inch index cards, colored pens or pencils, and pictures from magazines, tourist brochures, etc.

Portfolio Item Students should include in their portfolios their brainstorming list and first draft, as well as the final copy of their postcard.

Oral: Activity 33

Expanded Activity Divide students into three groups: a group of hosts (restaurant customers who have invited a friend for lunch), a group of guests (the invited friends), and a group of waiters and waitresses. Write down the names of the students in each group for later use. Have students read the five steps of Activity 33 and list the functional expressions and phrases they will need for each situation. Go over the phrases with each group to check for errors or pronunciation difficulties. Regroup students, putting a waiter, a host, and a guest in each group. Give students time to practice all five steps of Activity 33. As homework, tell students to review the functions and phrases that are necessary for their roles so that they will be prepared to role-play the situations spontaneously the following day. The next day, have restaurant props set up at the front of the class. Create groups immediately before each performance by randomly drawing names from the groups of hosts, guests, and waiters formed the previous day.

Purpose To give students an opportunity to practice functional expressions and vocabulary appropriate in a restaurant setting before having to produce language spontaneously.

Rationale Giving students an opportunity to practice language and then use it spontaneously in a real-life situation will help them internalize the functional expressions and vocabulary necessary in that situation.

Materials You will need restaurant props, such as a table covered with a cloth, two chairs, cutlery, plates and glasses, a tray and pad for the waiter, and a menu. You will also need audio or video equipment and cassettes.

Portfolio Item Record the performances on audio- or videocassette for incorporation into students' portfolios.

KAPITEL 7 Zu Hause helfen

Portfolio Suggestions

Written: Zum Lesen Activity 9

Expanded Activity Have pairs of students brainstorm and list the chores they do around the house and how often they have to do them. Then, with the whole class, discuss any new vocabulary and think of possible situations in which they might offer such help to a friend. Give students time to organize their letters and prepare a first draft, and then have them exchange letters for peer editing. Students should write their final drafts on letter paper or stationery.

Purpose To transfer information learned in the reading. The targeted functions are expressing obligations, talking about how often you have to do things, and offering help.

Rationale Students need to learn to approach writing as a process.

Materials Students will need letter paper or stationery.

Portfolio Item Students should include their notes from brainstorming and their first drafts, as well as the final copy of their letters in their portfolios.

Oral: Activity 29

Expanded Activity Students work in pairs to create one segment of a complete television newscast. The newscast could include stories about students' interests and activities, cafeteria food, fashion trends, and a weather report and forecast. Assign or let pairs choose the segment of the newscast they will work on. Allow time for students to plan, write, and practice their reports as well as prepare any props they might need (a weather map, for example). On the day before the newscast, plan the order of the program and let each pair know where their report falls in the program.

Purpose To practice functional expressions introduced in this chapter and review functions learned earlier. The targeted functions are talking about how often you have to do things and talking about weather.

Rationale Students need to use their new language in increasingly longer and more complicated contexts, even if it means making more mistakes.

Materials Students will need butcher paper or poster board, colored markers, and a pointer. You will also need video or audio equipment and cassettes.

Portfolio Item Record the newscast on audio- or videocassette for incorporation into students' portfolios.

Einkaufen gehen

Portfolio Suggestions

Written: Zum Lesen Activity 10

Expanded Activity The whole class works together to write an article about the new snack bar. After deciding on a name for the snack bar and a general menu, divide the class into three groups, each of which will be responsible for one part of the article. Each group writes two or three sentences about a specific aspect of the snack bar. One group will describe the decor, another group will write about the food served, and the third group will write about the prices. Elicit the sentences from each group and write them on the board. Together, the class will write an introduction and conclusion and make necessary corrections to the article.

Purpose To transfer information and vocabulary from the reading.

Rationale Students learn a great deal from each other as they work together to write an article.

Materials No special materials are necessary.

Portfolio Item Students each write a copy of the article for incorporation into their portfolios.

Oral: Anwendung Activity 3

Expanded Activity Have groups of students prepare radio or TV commercials advertising the snack bar they created in the written activity. They should focus on the same points that were described in the article: decor, menu, and price. Remind students to use **denn**- and **weil**-clauses to convince the audience to come to their snack bar.

Purpose To practice being persuasive and giving reasons while reviewing the vocabulary from this chapter. The targeted functions are telling someone what to do and giving reasons.

Rationale Students are able to manipulate a broad range of language and vocabulary in creative activities such as TV commercials.

Materials Students will need props such as menus, food items, and other items found at a snack bar. You will also need video or audio equipment and cassettes.

Portfolio Item Record the commercials on audio- or videocassette for incorporation in students' portfolios.

Amerikaner in München

Portfolio Suggestions

Written: Anwendung Activity 4

Expanded Activity Students write a letter to a German-speaking pen pal in which they tell about places to visit and things to do in their city or town and their opinion of these places. Students begin by brainstorming and listing things in their town that might be interesting to a visitor, such as sights, restaurants, and landmarks. They each choose at least two things of which they have a positive opinion and two of which they have a negative opinion to write about in their letter. Students should write their final drafts on stationery.

Purpose To practice writing personal opinions and review the chapter vocabulary in a realistic context and format. The targeted function is expressing opinions.

Rationale Students can generally communicate more effectively about a topic they are familiar with and about which they have already formed an opinion.

Materials Students will need letter paper or stationery.

Portfolio Item Brainstorming notes, early drafts, and the final copy of the letter should be included in the portfolio.

Oral: Anwendung Activity 5

Expanded Activity Divide students into pairs. Each pair decides on three locations from which they want another pair of students to buy something (bakery, post office, butcher shop, etc.). They then make up a series of directions from any starting point to the mystery locations. Each pair gives these directions orally to another pair. The pair receiving the directions follows them on the map, asking questions when necessary, and then decides on one item to buy when they reach each destination. (Example: **Wir sind jetzt beim Metzger und kaufen Bratwurst.**)

Purpose To practice giving and following directions. The targeted functions are talking about where something is located, and asking for and giving directions.

Rationale This is a good opportunity for students to practice using the second person plural in a realistic situation.

Materials Students will need the map of Mittersendling from page 253 of the *Pupil's Edition*. You will also need audio or video equipment and cassettes.

Portfolio Item Record the interaction between groups on audio- or videocassette for incorporation in the portfolios.

Kino und Konzerte

Portfolio Suggestions

Written: Zum Lesen Activity 8

Expanded Activity Elicit from students the names of movies they have seen recently. Choose four or five movies that most of the students have seen and divide students into groups, assigning each group a film that all of them have seen. Each group discusses their film together and makes notes about it, including the type of movie it is, the names of the actors, what they liked and disliked about it, etc. The discussion should help students remember details, use new vocabulary, and talk about several aspects of the film. After they have discussed the film thoroughly, the group collaborates to write a review of the movie. When they have written the review, each group shares their review with the class.

Purpose To practice writing about and explaining likes and dislikes, using vocabulary that enables students to talk about favorite movies and stars.

Rationale Using the new language to communicate real information about a relevant subject is motivating for students.

Materials No special materials are necessary.

Portfolio Item A copy of the group review goes in each member's portfolio.

Oral: Activity 24

Expanded Activity Students each prepare a one-to-two-minute review of a favorite book, video, cassette, or compact disc. The review should include the title and a brief description of the item, as well as a recommendation that others read, watch, or listen to it. Students should be encouraged to use notes but not to read from a prepared script as they deliver their review.

Purpose To give students a real context for practicing the targeted functions of expressing likes and dislikes, and expressing preferences and favorites.

Rationale Giving students the opportunity to talk about things that have personal meaning will motivate them to communicate in the new language.

Materials Students will need audio or video equipment and cassettes.

Portfolio Item Record students' reviews on audio- or videocassette for incorporation into the portfolio.

# Der Geburtstag

Portfolio Suggestions

Written: Activity 16

Expanded Activity To make this activity more authentic, you may want to have your students actually plan a party to which they invite other German classes from your school or other schools in your area, parents, or members of a local German **Verein** (see Oral Portfolio Suggestion, Chapter 12). Students should decide together the date, time, location, and contact person for the party before designing their invitations. The completed invitations can be distributed to guests who are being invited to the party.

Purpose To practice writing a friend, planning a social occasion, and making a schedule.

Rationale Using the new language to plan parties and get-togethers with friends makes learning fun and increases student interest.

Materials Students will need paper, scissors, tape, glue, and colored pens or pencils.

Portfolio Item If the invitations are distributed to potential party guests, be sure to make a copy for incorporation in the portfolio.

Oral: Activity 9

Expanded Activity On slips of paper, write activities students might invite each other to do (Examples: **ins Kino gehen, tanzen gehen, einkaufen gehen**) and put them into a "hat." Prepare another "hat" with slips of paper on which you have written "accept" or "decline." Have a pair of students sit in chairs you have set up back-to-back and each pick a slip of paper from one of the hats. The one who gets the paper with an activity on it initiates the phone call and invites the other student to do that activity. The second student either accepts or declines depending on the cue he or she received. Remind students to begin and end their conversation according to German custom.

Purpose To practice making phone calls. The targeted functions are using the telephone in Germany, inviting someone to an event of some kind, and accepting or declining an invitation.

Rationale Talking on the phone is difficult because communication must be spontaneous and visual clues such as body language and eye contact are not possible. This exercise will help students practice the skills necessary for authentic phone conversations.

Materials You will need two telephones to use as props, two chairs set up back-to-back about 2 to 3 feet apart, and audio or video equipment and cassettes.

Portfolio Item Record the telephone conversations on audio- or videocassette.

KAPITEL 12  Die Fete (Wiederholungskapitel)

Portfolio Suggestions

Written: Anwendung Activity 2

Expanded Activity Have students write a five-line poem about their favorite person based on the following procedure: For line one, write a noun that you associate with the person. For line two, write two adjectives that describe him or her. For line three, write three infinitives you associate with the person. For line four, write a statement about that person. For line five, write the person's name. Encourage students to write their final poems on nice paper and to illustrate or decorate them in some way.

Purpose To practice describing a person in a creative way.

Rationale Students will be empowered when they realize they are able to use the language they have learned so far to write a simple poem.

Materials Students will need letter paper and colored pens or pencils.

Portfolio Item Initial notes and drafts, as well as the final poem, can be incorporated into the portfolios.

Oral: Activity 6b

Expanded Activity Plan an actual party with your students, discussing all details in German. Together, choose a date, time, theme, and location for your party. Decide whether you will actually invite guests and if so, who they will be. Discuss what needs to be done and who will do it. Make sure that every student takes part in the planning and has something for which he or she is going to be responsible.

Purpose To practice planning an event, discussing the details of food, clothes, music, location, and guests for a party.

Rationale Taking part in the planning of a real party will help students synthesize and review many of the functions learned in Level 1 in a real-life situation.

Materials Students will need whatever they decide is necessary for their party. You will also need audio or visual equipment and cassettes.

Portfolio Item Record the class planning session for incorporation into the portfolio. You may also want to make someone responsible for filming the party as an end-of-year souvenir.

Performance Assessment

KAPITEL 1: Wer bist du?

Performance Assessment

Erste Stufe

Write the following statements on a transparency or on the board. Have students form the question that would elicit each statement as an answer. This can be done orally or in writing.

1. Ich heiße Martin. (Wie heißt du?)
2. Er heißt Hans. (Wie heißt er / der Junge / der Mann?)
3. Das ist die Nina. (Wer ist das?)
4. Sie heißt Frau Siegel. (Wie heißt sie / die Frau?)
5. Nein, er heißt Thomas. (Heißt er (Peter)? / Heißt der Junge (Peter)?)
6. Das ist Herr Heppt. (Wer ist das?)
7. Das ist die Monika. (Wer ist das?)
8. Ja, er heißt Stefan. (Heißt er / der Junge Stefan?)
9. Sie heißt Lise. (Wie heißt sie / das Mädchen / die Frau?)
10. Das ist Frau Schleifer, die Englischlehrerin. (Wer ist das?)

Zweite Stufe

On a transparency show the following sentence fragments and call on students to form complete sentences. You might also have students write several answers in full sentences on the chalkboard. Then correct sentences on the board if there are any mistakes.

ich	ist	15
du	bin	14
er	bist	16
sie (pl.)	sind	12
Peter		13
Maria		
sie		

Dritte Stufe

Ask one student to tell where he or she is from using the verb **kommen**. Then ask another student to repeat what the first student said using the verb **sein**. Repeat this activity with several students.

Example:
Student A: **Ich komme aus Dallas.**
Student B: **Sie ist aus Dallas.**

Global Assessment: Anwendung Activity 8

Have your students introduce the "exchange students" on page 31 of the *Pupil's Edition*.

First, they should get together in pairs or groups and prepare the statements they will use in their introductions. As much information as possible should be given about each exchange student, including name, age, place of origin, and the means by which he or she gets to school. Any additional information provided by the exchange students should also be included.

When all groups have finished, call on each of them to introduce one or more of the exchange students. You may want to have them use the pictures from the book as props.

KAPITEL 2 Spiel und Spaß

Performance Assessment

Erste Stufe

Give each student a piece of paper with the name of a well-known athlete or musician on it. Call on the individual students and ask them to tell the rest of the class who their person is and what he or she does. (Example: **Andre Agassi spielt Tennis.**)

You can turn this activity into a guessing game, if you wish, by asking the student to use a pronoun in place of the person's name. (Example: **Er spielt Tennis.**) The rest of the class should then attempt to figure out who the person is.

Zweite Stufe

Divide the class into two groups and put a Tic-Tac-Toe game on the chalkboard or on a transparency. Have teams take turns creating complete sentences or questions using the verbs in their correct forms. If a team is able to make a correct statement or question with a particular verb, that team can mark an X or an O in that space.

machen	fahren	joggen
schwimmen	tanzen	besuchen
~~sammeln~~	(schreiben)	spielen

X: **Ich sammle Briefmarken.**
O: **Wir schreiben Briefe.**

Dritte Stufe

Check students' comprehension by calling out the following sentences and having students respond with either **stimmt** or **stimmt nicht**.

Am Wochenende gehen wir gern in die Schule.
Die Deutschen spielen sehr gern Fußball.
Unsere (Basketball)mannschaft ist Spitze!
Wir schwimmen gern im Winter.
Ich finde Schach toll.
Wir machen im Sommer Hausaufgaben.
Ich besuche meine Freunde gern.

Global Assessment: Anwendung Activity 8

Have students get together in groups of three to make a plan about how they would like to spend some of their free time together. They should pretend that school has just ended on Friday afternoon, and that they have met to decide on what they would like to do next. They will need to discuss the activities that each member of the group likes and dislikes in order to find several that are agreeable to all. Once they have decided which activities they would all enjoy, they should discuss when they would like to do them. When all groups have finished, have them report their plans to the class.

Komm mit nach Hause!

Performance Assessment

Erste Stufe

Have students form groups of three to role-play an afternoon gathering at someone's house. The host should offer a variety of snacks and beverages. The two guests should take some time to decide what they would like, asking about the choices before they make up their minds.

Zweite Stufe

Have students prepare a short oral description of the furniture in their bedroom at home. They should describe the contents of the room as well as the size, level of comfort, and attractiveness of the furniture.

Dritte Stufe

Ask students to describe orally or in writing:

a) a fantasy girlfriend or boyfriend (what would he or she look and be like?)
b) their best friend.

Students must give the name and age and describe the physical appearance, the interests, and the likes and dislikes of the person they choose.

Global Assessment: Anwendung Activity 9

Students should form groups of three in order to role-play a situation that takes place one day after school. One student, the host, has invited two friends over for the afternoon. First, the host should offer his or her friends something to eat and drink, and afterward show the guests his or her room. Some changes have recently been made to the room, which the three friends discuss. Afterward, the conversation turns to family; each student describes various family members, what they look like, and what their interests are.

Students should write out and practice their conversations before presenting them to the class. You may want to videotape the performances.

KAPITEL 4 — Alles für die Schule!

Performance Assessment

Erste Stufe

Draw a five-day **Stundenplan** on the board. Call it **Dieters Stundenplan.** Write the German names of all the subjects learned in this **Stufe** on large index cards. Put masking tape on the back of the cards so you can attach them to the chalkboard. Tell individual students to put the subject cards in their correct places on the **Stundenplan** according to your directions. Use sequencing words as well as times in your directions. Example: **Am Montag hat Dieter zuerst Englisch.** Call on different students for each new sentence until you complete the **Stundenplan.**

Zweite Stufe

Have all students stand up. Give several quick commands based on material introduced in this **Stufe**. Example: **Wenn dein Lieblingsfach Deutsch ist, setz dich, bitte! Wenn du Englisch um (8 Uhr 30) hast, schreib deinen Namen an die Tafel!** If anybody is left standing after your series of commands, your last command should be: **Setz dich, wenn du heute Deutsch hast!**

Dritte Stufe

Collect examples of all the school supplies discussed in this chapter and place them around the room. For each item make an index card with an approximate German price on it and tape it underneath the item. Ask students a two-part question for each labeled item.

Example: **Wo sind die Taschenrechner? Und wie viel kostet der Taschenrechner?**
Example: **Sie sind dort drüben. Er kostet 16 Euro.**

Global Assessment: Anwendung Activity 9

Students should assemble in groups of three to write out the script for a conversation that takes place in a school supply store. The students should pretend that they meet by accident at the store, after which they begin to talk about the following subjects:

a) what classes they have and when
b) which classes they like and dislike, and their favorite classes
c) their grades in some of their classes (their friends should respond appropriately to this news)

For the second part of the role-playing activity, you should assume the role of the salesperson in the store and have the students ask you about the location and cost of various supplies.

Once students have had time to write out and rehearse their scripts, have them perform their scenario for the class.

KAPITEL 5: Klamotten kaufen

Performance Assessment

Erste Stufe

For this activity you will need a spinning color wheel that can be made from paper plates with paper fasteners. Spin the wheel and ask the students to name the color on which the wheel stops. Ask any students wearing something in that color to name that article of clothing.

Example: If the wheel landed on blue, one student might say, **Meine Jacke ist blau, und meine Socken sind auch blau.**

Zweite Stufe

Ask students to comment on two articles of clothing they are wearing that day.

Example: **Ich finde das Hemd prima.**
Die Hose ist zu kurz.

Dritte Stufe

Ask individual students to follow in pantomime various commands using the verbs **nehmen, geben, anziehen,** or **anprobieren** and the clothing vocabulary.

Example: **Marjorie, zieh den Rock an!**

Global Assessment: Anwendung Activity 7

Have students form groups of three and role-play a situation in which one of them is attempting to find something to wear to a party.

In the first part of the conversation, the friends are at home. One tries on various different types of clothes, but cannot find anything that fits or is the right color. The other two friends comment on the clothes.

In the second part of the conversation, the friends have decided to go to the store to buy something new for the party. Here, one student needs to play a salesperson, while the other two assume the role of customer. The students should select one of the two display windows in Activity 2, page 152 of the *Pupil's Edition* upon which to base their conversation. The two in the role of customer should ask for various items in specific colors; the salesperson will let them know what is and is not available. The student searching for a new outfit should try on several different articles of clothing, while the friend and the salesperson comment on the look and fit of the clothes. Your students can end the scenario either by having the student find something he or she likes, or by leaving the store without buying anything.

When students have written out their conversations and had time to practice them, they should act them out for the class using props. You may want to videotape the performances.

KAPITEL 6 Pläne machen

Performance Assessment

Erste Stufe

Show students two cards: one with an activity (Example: **zur Schule gehen**), and one with a time (Example: **7.45**). Have them build sentences by putting the two together: **Um Viertel vor acht gehe ich zur Schule.** You might then have them tell you whether the sentence they created applies to them personally, using the words **stimmt** and **stimmt nicht**.

Zweite Stufe

Make up envelopes with sentence strips ahead of time, using the sentences from Activity 20 on p.167 or your own original sentences. Distribute the envelopes to students and ask them to use the pieces to form sentences using correct word order. Monitor students' work and ask several students to read their sentences aloud.

Dritte Stufe

Ask students to look back at the **Imbisskarte** on page 170. Playing the role of the waitperson, ask individual students what they would like to order. Have students "order" one or two items, ask them how each item tastes, and then move on to the next student.

Global Assessment: Anwendung Activity 6

Have your students pair up and pretend that they have decided to drop by an **Imbissstand** for a snack. (You might want to have them use the menu on page 181 of the *Pupil's Edition* as a prop.)

In the first part of the conversation, the students should discuss the foods that are available at the snack stand, and each should decide what he or she wants to eat and drink. They're all on tight budgets and can't afford to spend more than 5 euros each; therefore, they next need to figure out how much their choices will cost.

Once they've decided upon snacks they can afford, have students take turns in the roles of vendor and customer, so that each can order the food and drink he or she decided upon. After the students order and receive their food, make sure they remember to pay for it!

When the students have had adequate time to write and rehearse their scripts, have them perform their scenario for the class. You may want to film their performances.

Zu Hause helfen

Performance Assessment

Erste Stufe

Extend invitations to individual students to sightsee in Munich. Students should decline each invitation, giving a reason (preferably a chore) why they cannot go.

Zweite Stufe

Conduct a survey addressing the functions introduced in this **Stufe**. Ask individual students questions related to chores around the house. Example: **Wie oft musst du Staub saugen? Was machst du nicht gern zu Hause? Wann mähst du den Rasen? Musst du ein Haustier füttern?**

Dritte Stufe

As students walk into the classroom, hand some of them small index cards with the following information: name of a city, current weather conditions, and temperature. Once the class gets underway, call on students to report their information in German.

Global Assessment: Anwendung Activity 6

Have students form groups of three or four and write a script for the following role-playing activity:

It's a rainy day, and one student is at home doing chores when his or her friends show up and offer to help. The first student tells them what help is needed. As everyone gets busy, another student makes a suggestion about where they should all go during their free time the next day. As they discuss possible destinations, a great crash of thunder turns the conversation to the next day's weather. They talk about how the weather will be, and decide on tomorrow's activity.

When students have had time to write and practice their scripts, have them act out their scenarios for the class. They should use various props to convey the idea of doing chores around the house. You may want to film their performances.

Kapitel 8: Einkaufen gehen

Performance Assessment

Erste Stufe

Have the following information listed on a transparency you have prepared ahead of time. List four different kinds of stores and at least three items per store.

Metzger	Bäcker	Obst- und Gemüseladen	Schreibwarenladen
Wurst	Kuchen	Äpfel	Kuli
...	...	...	...

Show the transparency to the class for one minute as you go over the words and review the vocabulary. Then turn off the overhead and call on students to list as many items as they can remember.

Zweite Stufe

Divide the class into groups of three. Each group should have a writer, a checker, and a reporter. Tell groups that they are responsible for making a grocery list and a menu for an upcoming party they are giving together. Give each group a number of friends to invite. Each group will decide what foods to serve at the party. They also need to determine the quantities for each item to be purchased. The writer then makes out the shopping list as well as an outline for the menu. The checker proofreads the assignment, and the reporter tells the class the **Einkaufsliste** and menu for the upcoming event.

Dritte Stufe

Ask students to tell you what they bought the last time they went shopping. They should use the expression **habe ... gekauft**.

Global Assessment: Anwendung Activity 6

Have students pair up and write a script for the following two scenes:

a) The two students are preparing lunch, and decide to make an **Obstsalat**. (Students can either make up their own recipe for the salad, or use the one on page 241 of the *Pupil's Edition*.) They should discuss what ingredients are necessary, how much of each is required, and where they should go to get them. One student should write up a shopping list.

b) The second scene takes place at the store, where one student arrives with the list in hand and the other plays the salesperson. The salesperson should ask the customer what he or she needs, how much is required, and whether he or she needs anything else. The customer buys the necessary ingredients and leaves the store.

Have students rehearse their scripts and then act them out for the class using props brought from home. You may want to videotape their performances.

Amerikaner in München

Performance Assessment

Erste Stufe

Make a list of landmarks and locations in your town or city using the **Wortschatz** expressions of this **Stufe**. (Examples: **Kirche, Rathaus**) Ask students to tell the location of each item in German.

Zweite Stufe

Prepare a set of index cards with a location from Transparency 9-1 written on each. Have two students, A and B, come to the front of the room and draw a card each. Student A's location is the starting point, and Student B must guide him or her to Location B. Have Student A go to the overhead projector and trace with his or her finger the oral directions given by Student B. Once Student A reaches Location B, the two students should draw new cards and switch roles. New pairs should be called forward until all students have given and followed directions.

Dritte Stufe

Make a town out of the classroom, using rows between desks as streets. You can label the streets by laying signs on the floor. Signs indicating different locations in the city (**Kirche, Postamt**) can be placed on desks throughout the room. Then call on students to role-play a situation. Starting at the front of the classroom (or any other suitable point), a student asks for directions to a location you select at random. That student follows directions given by classmates as he or she moves around the make-believe city.

Global Assessment: Anwendung Activity 7

Have your students assemble in groups of three or four. First, they should design a menu for an **Imbissstube** and write it on a piece of paper or poster board. Then they need to write a script for and role-play the following two-part situation, taking place at a snack stand:

a) The friends arrive at the snack stand, at which one of their number will need to play the role of the salesperson. Those students acting as customers should look at the menu and discuss what's available. Each should then order something, ask what it costs, and pay the person behind the counter. Make sure the students carry out the exchanges politely!

b) The students then discuss how the food tastes, and whether or not someone wants more. If so, they should return to the counter and order more. To wrap up the scenario, the students should discuss their opinions about the city of Munich, which they have been visiting that day.

When students have finished their scripts and had sufficient time to rehearse them, have them perform for the class. You may want to videotape their performances.

Kino und Konzerte

Performance Assessment

Erste Stufe

Ask students to give a description and a short critique of the last movie they saw in a movie theater or on video.

Zweite Stufe

Write a list of current movies or popular songs on the board. Ask individual students to give one reason why someone should or should not see a particular movie or listen to a specific song.

Dritte Stufe

Write the titles of several well-known novels on the board. Call on students individually, asking them questions using the verbs **lesen** and **sprechen** and requesting that they use a title from the board in their answers. (Examples: **Was liest du jetzt auf Englisch? Worüber sprecht ihr heute? Was lesen deine Klassenkameraden am liebsten?**) Follow these questions by asking students to categorize the books listed. (Example: **Was für ein Buch ist** *Fahrenheit 451*?)

Global Assessment: Anwendung Activity 7

Have students get together in groups of three or four to write a script for one of the following situations:

a) The students are standing in front of a movie theater and want to see a film. They should talk about the different movies that are showing there and discuss which ones they expect they'll like, dislike, and strongly dislike, as well as about which one(s) they have already seen. Together they should decide which movie they will watch.

b) The students are at a video store to rent **(ausleihen)** a movie. They talk about what kinds of movies each likes and which ones they've already seen, and end by deciding on a movie that everyone will enjoy.

When students have finished preparing their scripts and have had time to rehearse them, have them perform their scenario for the class. You may want to videotape the performances.

KAPITEL 11 Der Geburtstag

Performance Assessment

Erste Stufe

This activity should be conducted with students individually, if time allows. Ask individual students to dramatize the following situations in mini-skits: You (the student) call a friend at home. You find out that he or she is not home so you give your name and phone number. Ask when your friend will be back and leave a message. Say you would like your call returned before 9:00 p.m., if possible.

Zweite Stufe

Go around the class and ask individual students questions to which they have to respond by giving specific days, dates, and months. Vary questions.

Example: Sam, wann feiern wir dieses Jahr Thanksgiving?
Welches Datum haben wir heute?
Welches Datum war gestern?

Dritte Stufe

As students enter the class, give each one an index card with the name of a famous person written on it. Once class gets underway, ask students what they would give that person on his or her birthday.

Global Assessment: Anwendung Activity 6

Have your students assemble in groups of three or four. Each group should pick a type of store that the class has learned about (**Metzgerei, Modegeschäft, Schreibwarenladen ...**) and write it on a card. All the cards should be put in a box, from which a representative from each group will then draw a card. Students should pretend that the store on their new card has hired their group to write a commercial to help boost their sales for the holidays. The members of each group will collaborate to write a script for the commercial, in which they will try to convince people to buy the store's wares as gifts. They might want to suggest people in the family to whom their products could be given as gifts. (The group that drew the **Metzgerei** card will have to be particularly persuasive!)

When students have finished writing their scripts and have had time to practice them, have them perform their commercials for the class. You may wish to videotape the performances.

KAPITEL 12 Die Fete (Wiederholungskapitel)

Performance Assessment

Erste Stufe

- Ask students to give directions or describe the path they take from their bedroom to the refrigerator in the kitchen for a midnight snack. Ask them to describe what they would choose for their midnight snack.

- Have students invent a dish that contains all of the following ingredients: **Zwiebeln, Zitronen, Öl, Salz, Zimt,** and **Butterschmalz.** They can combine these ingredients with any other foods whose German names they have learned this year. When they have finished with their list, they should make up a German name for their new dish.

Zweite Stufe

Put the following expressions on the board: **ins Kino gehen; ins Theater gehen; Schlittschuh laufen gehen; zu einer Fete gehen; die Stadt besichtigen.** Then ask students to describe what they would wear for each of these activities.

Dritte Stufe

Give each student a piece of paper on which you have written the name of a book, movie, TV show, or an item which could have been bought. (Examples: *Star Wars*®, *Les Misérables,* **ein Pulli, eine Stereoanlage**) Then ask students individually what they did at some point in the past. (Example: **Kim, was hast du gestern Abend gemacht?**) The students should respond based on the information on their cards. For example, a student with the card **"ein Pulli"** would respond **Ich habe einen Pulli gekauft.** Next, ask each student a follow-up question leading him or her to describe the item (book, film, show) in some way. Example: **Wie sieht dein Pulli aus?** or **Wie war der Film?**

Global Assessment: Anwendung Activity 6

Have students prepare for this activity a day or two ahead of time by brainstorming a name for a German clothing store and deciding what sorts of clothes will be sold there. Tell them to bring a few examples of those kinds of clothes with them on the day scheduled for the following activity. (This activity can also be used as an expansion of Activity 16 on page 345.)

Have each student write out on a slip of paper the name he or she decided upon for the clothing store. Collect them all in a box and draw out five at random. The students whose stores were chosen should line up at the front of the class with the clothes they brought along and play the role of **Verkäufer(innen).** The rest of the class will divide into pairs and take turns visiting the stores on the **Einkaufsstraße.** Students should ask the salespeople about color and price, try some of the clothes on, and discuss the fit of the clothes. The second student of each pair should comment about the other's choice when he or she tries something on.

When the students have finished with the first five stores, draw more store names and have the class continue its shopping spree.

German 1 Komm mit!   Alternative Assessment Guide

CD-ROM Assessment

KAPITEL 1: Wer bist du?

DISC 1

CD-ROM Assessment

Guided Recording

Zum Sprechen
Students record a conversation by responding to the following video prompts:

1. Hallo. Ich heiße Katja. Und du? Wie heißt du?
2. Wie alt bist du?
3. Woher kommst du denn?
4. Ich komme mit dem Rad zur Schule. Wie kommst du zur Schule?
5. Also, bis dann. Tschüs!

Guided Writing

Zum Schreiben
Students choose from among the following four writing scenarios:

E-mail You're contacting a Swiss boy on an Internet key pal network. Write him an e-mail message telling him your name, age, where you're from, and how you get to school. Then ask him his age, where he's from, and how he gets to school.

Survey As an exchange student in Germany, you've noticed that your German classmates get to school many different ways. Make a survey listing all the ways you think German students get to school so you can find out more and tell your classmates back home about it.

Letter You're in Germany as an exchange student and are sending a letter back home to your classmates with some photos of new friends. Write about your friends, the people pictured above, remembering to tell who each person is, what his or her name and age are, and where he or she is from.

Conversation Imagine you're going to be an exchange student in Germany. Write a conversation in which you're meeting a new friend on your first day in school. Remember to greet your friend, ask his or her name and give yours, ask his or her age and give yours, and talk about where you're both from.

> Encourage students to use the online resources, such as the Vocabulary ("W") and the Grammar Summary ("G"), when working on their assignments. These resources may be accessed from the navigation bar at the bottom of the screen. Some students may also want to use their textbooks as a reference.

Spiel und Spaß

KAPITEL 2 — DISC 1

CD-ROM Assessment

Guided Recording

Zum Sprechen

Students record a conversation by responding to the following video prompts:

1. Spielst du ein Instrument?
2. Ich spiele gern Fußball. Du auch? Was spielst du gern?
3. Hast du auch andere Interessen?
4. Was machst du nach der Schule?
5. Was machst du am Wochenende?

Guided Writing

Zum Schreiben

Students choose from among the following four writing scenarios:

E-mail Your Austrian key pal has sent you a message telling you about his interests. The following is part of his message:

Und ich spiele sehr gern Fußball und Volleyball. Aber Tennis spiele ich nicht so gern. Nach der Schule höre ich oft Musik mit Freunden. Ich spiele auch Klavier. Und du, spielst du ein Instrument? Was machst du in deiner Freizeit? Schreib mir bald! Otto

Answer Otto's message by telling him about what you like to do. Be sure to include at least three activities you do during the week and three you do on the weekend. Also, ask Otto's opinion of the activities you like to do.

Brochure Make a travel brochure listing activities that can be done at a recreational camp in Germany. Include six indoor and six outdoor activities. Be sure to add phrases expressing an opinion about certain activities to let people know it's fun to go there.

Survey Your Swiss pen pal is curious about which activities American teenagers like to do. Make a survey for your classmates to take, in which they will give their opinion of ten different activities.

Note Your friend from Liechtenstein thinks guitar music is cool and is interested in taking lessons. She passed you a note telling you that she would like for you to take lessons with her. Write her a note, telling her if you have the same opinion about guitars. Also, tell about all the things you usually do after school, in the evening, and on the weekend, to see if there's a time you could both take the lessons.

Encourage students to use the online resources, such as the Vocabulary ("W") and the Grammar Summary ("G"), when completing their assignments. These resources may be accessed from the navigation bar at the bottom of the screen. Some students may also want to use their textbooks as a reference.

KAPITEL 3 — Komm mit nach Hause!
DISC 1

CD-ROM Assessment

Guided Recording

Zum Sprechen

Students record a conversation between a host or hostess and a guest based on the following written prompts:

Host/Hostess Ask your guest what he or she would like to drink.

Guest Ask your host or hostess politely for a glass of mineral water.

Host/Hostess Ask if your guest would like a piece of cake.

Guest Politely decline the offer.

Host/Hostess Ask your guest to describe his or her brother to you.

Guest Say your brother is 15, has short blond hair, and green eyes.

Guided Writing

Zum Schreiben

Students choose from among the following writing scenarios:

List A friend of yours who doesn't speak German is going to Germany on vacation. Create a list to take along that includes three ways to say thank you and three ways to say please or you're welcome.

E-mail You're contacting a girl from Switzerland on an Internet pen pal network. Write her an e-mail message telling her about your family members, how old they are, and what they look like. Tell her also about your pets. Then ask if she has brothers and sisters, how old they are, and what they look like. Remember to ask her if she has pets, too, and what their names are.

Postcard As an exchange student in Germany, you are surprised to find out how different your host friend's bedroom looks. Write a postcard to your classmates describing the furniture in the room.

Journal entry Imagine you're going to be an exchange student in Austria. In your journal, write four questions you would want to ask your host friend about his or her family and pets.

KAPITEL 4 — Alles für die Schule!

DISC 1

CD-ROM Assessment

Guided Recording

Zum Sprechen

Students record a conversation between a customer and a salesperson based on the following written prompts:

Customer Politely ask the salesperson where the notebooks and pens are.

Salesperson Tell your customer the notebooks and pens are in the back.

Customer Ask the salesperson where you can find calculators.

Salesperson Tell your customer that the calculators are up front and cost 10,50.

Customer Tell the salesperson you think the calculators are pretty expensive, and ask about the price of school bags.

Salesperson Tell your customer that the school bags are really a bargain and how much they cost.

Guided Writing

Zum Schreiben

Students choose from among the following four writing scenarios:

Schedule Create your ideal class schedule. Include all of the classes you would like to have and the days and times you might have them.

Conversation Imagine and write a conversation in which a German teenager, Dieter, talks about school with his grandmother. She asks him about when his classes are, which ones he likes and doesn't like, and which subject is his favorite. Finally, she asks him about his grades. He tells her about some good and bad grades as she reacts to the news.

Commercial Write the script for a commercial for Schul-Shop Kaut-Bulling & Co. In your script, a customer should ask the salesperson about the prices of different school supplies. The customer should make positive comments about the items and their prices.

Article Imagine that you're writing an article about German schools for your German club's newsletter. Include in your article what you've found out about a typical school schedule in Germany, what classes German teenagers have and like, and what kind of grades they receive.

German 1 Komm mit!   Alternative Assessment Guide   **49**

Klamotten kaufen

CD-ROM Assessment

Guided Recording

Zum Sprechen
Students record a conversation between a salesperson and a customer based on the following written prompts:

Salesperson Ask your customer what he or she would like.

Customer Tell the salesperson that you're looking for a red sweater in a specific size.

Salesperson Tell your customer that you have a sweater in that size, but it's in another color.

Customer Say you think the sweater is really stylish and you want to try it on. Ask if the salesperson thinks the sweater is too baggy.

Salesperson Tell your customer that the sweater looks great on. Tell him or her that it only costs 25,00.

Customer Say that you think it's expensive, but you'll take it.

Guided Writing

Zum Schreiben
Students choose from among the following four writing scenarios:

Survey Create a survey for your classmates to find out which clothes items are the most and least popular. Be sure to find out about color and fit of the items as well.

Conversation Create a conversation between a salesperson and a customer who is having trouble finding something he or she likes. The customer should try on several items, and the salesperson should comment on the fit, color, and the style of the clothing. Finally, the customer should find out how much the items cost and say what he or she will buy.

Note Write a note to your friends, Bianca and Ralf, to let them know what they should wear to a party you've invited them to next weekend. Tell them also why you're suggesting these outfits.

Magazine ad Create a magazine ad for the clothes store, MODE-WELT, telling which items of clothing the store sells. Be sure to mention the colors and sizes the clothes come in. Create slogans to help persuade people to buy the items. Include the hours and days the store is open as well. You may want to leave space for illustrations and add them after you've printed out your ad.

KAPITEL 6 — Pläne machen

DISC 2

CD-ROM Assessment

Guided Recording

Zum Sprechen

Students record a conversation by responding to the following video prompts:

1. Ich bekomme ein Glas Tee. Was trinkst du?
2. Hm... Ich glaube, ich nehme eine Nudelsuppe. Und was isst du?
3. So, wie schmeckt's?
4. Also, Martin und ich, wir gehen ins Kino. Wie spät ist es denn?
5. Also, ich muss jetzt nach Hause. Wo ist denn der Kellner? ... Hallo! Wir möchten zahlen. [KELLNER] Also, das macht zusammen 9 Euro 20.

Guided Writing

Zum Schreiben

Students choose from among the following four writing scenarios:

Letter In his last letter, your German pen pal, Theo, asked about what you and your friends like to do after school. Write him back, telling him what you usually do and at what times. Also tell him about four activities you want to do in the next month.

Menu The German club needs a menu for its café at the International Fair at school. Create a menu, including a name for the café, the food and drink items available, and the prices.

Script Write the script for a scene in a TV show in which several friends meet and make plans to go somewhere. They should greet each other and find out how things are going, and ask each other what they want to do. Once they've agreed on the activity, they should decide on a time.

Conversation Write the dialogue of a conversation that takes place in the Café Freizeit. First the customers should talk about what they want to eat and drink, then the waiter should take their order. Then the customers should talk about how the food tastes, and finally they should pay the check.

Before writing the conversation, have students use **An die Tasten!** to create a menu for Café Freizeit. Students might want to add illustrations after printing their work.

German 1 Komm mit! — Alternative Assessment Guide **51**

KAPITEL 7 — Zu Hause helfen

DISC 2

CD-ROM Assessment

Guided Recording

Zum Sprechen

Students record a conversation between two friends based on the following written prompts:

- **Student A** Tell your friend you can't go to the movies because you have to help around the house today.
- **Student B** Ask your friend what he or she has to do.
- **Student A** Tell your friend you have to wash the dishes, vacuum, and wash the windows.
- **Student B** Ask your friend how often he or she has to help around the house.
- **Student A** Tell your friend you have to help around the house three times a month. Ask if your friend wants to help you by cleaning the windows.
- **Student B** Tell your friend you'll do it.

Guided Writing

Zum Schreiben

Students choose from among the following four writing scenarios:

List of chores As a birthday present, three of your classmates have decided to help you do your chores this month. Make a list for each of them of all the chores you would like them to do during the next month.

Survey Create a survey to ask your classmates about how often they do various chores. Your survey should also ask respondents to rate how much they like or dislike each chore.

Conversation Kirsten has recently arrived to stay with an Austrian family for a year. Create a conversation between Kirsten, who would like to know what she can do to help around the house, and her host sister, Gabi, who has lots of chores she would like help with.

Travel guide Create an illustrated travel guide to inform tourists about the weather in several cities across Europe.

Have students follow these steps to complete their travel guide.

PREWRITING First, pick eight European cities. Then, brainstorm a list of all the words and expressions you know to describe weather conditions.

WRITING For each city you picked, write a 2-to-3 sentence paragraph describing what the weather is like, using the appropriate words and expressions from your PREWRITING list. Be sure to include temperatures for different months and the weather conditions of each season. Be sure to leave space for illustrations.

REVISING Print the text for your guide, make any necessary changes to improve it, and check it for correct spelling, umlauts, accents, and capitalization.

PUBLISHING Correct any errors, rewrite anything you need to for greater clarity or emphasis, and print a final copy of your work. Be sure to add illustrations or maps of the locations before turning in your travel guide.

Kapitel 8: Einkaufen gehen

CD-ROM Assessment — DISC 2

Guided Recording

Zum Sprechen

Students record a conversation between a salesperson and a customer at the butcher shop based on the following written prompts:

Salesperson Ask your customer what he or she would like to buy.
Customer Say that you need ground meat.
Salesperson Ask your customer how much ground meat he or she would like.
Customer Say that you need 500 grams of ground meat.
Salesperson Ask if your customer would like anything else.
Customer Say that you still need 200 grams of cold cuts and a chicken.

Guided Writing

Zum Schreiben

Students choose from among the following four writing scenarios:

E-mail message Your Swiss key pal is interested in knowing about what kinds of foods are served in your school's cafeteria. Send your key pal a message, telling her about a typical lunch menu for each day of the week.

Journal entry Imagine you've just done the grocery shopping with your host brother in Germany. Write down which shops you went to and what food items you bought there. Remember to include how much of each item you bought.

Conversation Michael is organizing a party for his best friend and needs help with the shopping and cleaning. Write the conversation between him and his brothers Heinz and Bruno. Heinz is very helpful and volunteers to do a lot, but Bruno only gives reasons for not helping.

TV commercial Write the script for a TV commercial advertising a new food market called Wertmarkt. The script of your commercial should include several customers purchasing items from a salesperson while making positive comments about the store.

KAPITEL 9 — Amerikaner in München
DISC 3

CD-ROM Assessment

Guided Recording

Zum Sprechen

Students record a conversation between an American student and a German police officer based on the following written prompts:

Student Ask the police officer if he or she knows where there is a snack bar and how you can get there.

Officer Tell the student to go straight ahead up to the traffic light and go right. Then, take the next street to the left.

Student Ask the officer if he or she knows what there is to eat there.

Officer Tell the student about two southern German specialties that they have there.

Student Ask the officer if he or she thinks the food there is good.

Officer Tell the student that you think the food is very good and always fresh there.

Guided Writing

Zum Schreiben

Students choose from among the following four writing scenarios:

Commercial Create the dialogue for a commercial for the **Imbissstube am Rathaus**. In your commercial, a tourist should ask the employee what there is to eat and drink. The employee should be sure to include any regional specialties they have to offer. Once the tourist has ordered, the employee should ask what he or she thinks of the food and if he or she would like more. The tourist should give a very positive opinion of the **Imbissstube**.

Itinerary Write an itinerary listing the places you would like and will need to go to during your first week in Munich.

Directions Some of your classmates are planning to travel to Munich soon. Since you've spent some time there, you're familiar with some places where they want to go. They've asked you to write down some directions for them to take along. Using the map above, write directions from the train station to a hotel, from the hotel to the Theatinerkirche, from the Theatinerkirche to City Hall, and from City Hall to the Nationaltheater.

Newspaper article You are a travel reporter for a magazine writing an article about the city of Munich. Write and give your opinion about some of the places there are to see and some of the local foods that there are to try in Munich.

Have students who choose to do the newspaper article use the Internet for their research. Tell students they can use keywords such as "Restaurants," "Sehenswürdigkeiten," "Museen," "Kirchen," or "Theater." When students have finished their research, have them organize their findings according to the categories 1) places to see and 2) restaurants to visit. For places to see, students should include everything there is to do and see there, and for restaurants to visit, they should include what food and house specialties are available.

Kapitel 10 — Kino und Konzerte

DISC 3

CD-ROM Assessment

Guided Recording

Zum Sprechen

Students record a conversation by responding to the following video prompts:

1. Klassische Musik mag ich sehr gern. Und was für Musik magst du?
2. Und Filme? Ich mag Abenteuerfilme und Sciencefictionfilme. Siehst du lieber Abenteuerfilme oder Sciencefictionfilme?
3. Aber am liebsten sehe ich Komödien, weil sie so lustig sind. Und du? Was siehst du am liebsten?
4. Kennst du den Schauspieler Keanu Reeves?
5. Am Wochenende habe ich mit Melina das Video von *Johnny Mnemonic* gesehen. Und du, hast du einen Film gesehen? Was hast du am Wochenende gemacht?

Guided Writing

Zum Schreiben

Students choose from among the following four writing scenarios:

Journal You stayed at home last weekend. Write a journal entry telling what you did, what you read, what videos or movies you saw, and how they were.

Dialogue Write a dialogue between two friends who are planning to rent a movie. They should tell each other which kinds of movies they prefer, and which ones they don't like at all and why. The two friends have very different tastes but finally agree on a movie.

Review The German class that you and your classmates correspond with is interested in knowing more about American music. Write a review of eight songs that are popular among your classmates. Be sure to tell the name of each song, what kind of music it is, who the singer is, and your personal opinion of the song.

Survey An Austrian exchange student is coming to visit your class next week. Since you're curious about what sort of music and movies speakers of German might like, make a list of ten questions to ask about the student's likes, dislikes, preferences, and favorites in music and movies.

Kapitel 11 · Disc 3: Der Geburtstag

CD-ROM Assessment

Guided Recording

Zum Sprechen

Students record a conversation with a partner based on the following written prompts:

Student A Ask your partner when Mother's Day is.

Student B Tell your partner that you think Mother's Day is on the 11th of May.

Student A Tell your partner that you'll buy your mother some chocolates or perfume. Then ask what your partner will buy for his or her mother.

Student B Tell your partner that you don't know yet and ask him or her for ideas.

Student A Suggest that your partner buy a bouquet of flowers or jewelry for his or her mother.

Student B Tell your partner you think it's a good idea and you'll do it.

Guided Writing

Zum Schreiben

Students choose from among the following four writing scenarios:

Note Write a note to four of your best friends inviting them to your birthday party. The note should include the day, date, and time of the party, as well as the reason for the party. Ask your friends to call you if they can come.

Greeting cards You've decided to make some greeting cards to send to your host family in Switzerland this year. Create text for four different occasions you think your host family might celebrate. When you've printed out the text, you might want to add appropriate illustrations to complete your cards.

List Tell when two of your family members and three of your friends have birthdays and write next to each date what you intend to give each person as a present.

Conversation Write the script of a telephone conversation between Elke and Bernd, discussing the upcoming Namenstag celebration of a mutual friend, Erich. Be sure to include phrases to start and finish the telephone call, as well as the date and time for the party, and what kind of gifts you plan to buy.

KAPITEL 12 Die Fete (Wiederholungskapitel)

DISC 3

CD-ROM Assessment

Guided Recording

Zum Sprechen
Students record a conversation by responding to the following video prompts:

1. Ich brauche einen Pulli, aber in Rot. Und du, was suchst du?
2. Ach, der Pulli dort drüben sieht sehr fesch aus. Ich probiere ihn an. Wie passt er? Was meinst du? Nicht zu lang oder zu eng?
3. Wirklich? Also, den Pulli finde ich toll. Ich nehme ihn. Sag, dein Bruder hat bald Geburtstag, nicht? Was schenkst du ihm?
4. Du weißt, meine Schwester hat nächste Woche Geburtstag. Ich weiß noch nicht, was ich ihr schenken will. Hmm... Hast du vielleicht eine Idee?
5. Prima Idee! Das mach ich! Oh, es ist schon Viertel nach zwei. Um halb drei gehe ich mit Freunden in den Zoo. Willst du mitkommen?

Guided Writing

Zum Schreiben
Students choose from among the following four writing scenarios:

Conversation Write the script of a telephone conversation in which Jens and Markus talk about their plans for the weekend. Markus has already made some plans, but he invites Jens to go along. Jens is also very busy this weekend, but finally decides to accept one of Markus' invitations.

Note Your Austrian exchange brother has agreed to do some chores and errands to help you get ready for a party. Write him a note telling him what he should do and what he should buy. Be sure to write directions for each place he'll need to go.

List Make a list of people to whom you plan to give gifts this year. Write what you plan to give each person and why.

Letter You've just received the address of your new German pen pal, Kirsten. Write her a letter describing yourself, your family, and where you're from.

Have students follow these steps to complete their letter.

PREWRITING First, brainstorm a list of all the words and expressions you know to describe or give information about each of the topics you'll include in your letter. Be sure to include where you're from, where you live, who your family members are and what they're like, what your room is like, and what you like to do.

WRITING For each topic, write a short paragraph, using the appropriate words and expressions from your PREWRITING list.

REVISING Print out your letter, make any necessary changes to improve it, and check it for correct spelling, umlauts, accents, and capitalization.

PUBLISHING Correct any errors, rewrite anything you need to for greater clarity or emphasis, and print a final copy of your letter.